Thoughts
along the Way

Silina Flacks

AuthorHouse™
1663 Liberty Drive
Bloomington, IN 47403
www.authorhouse.com
Phone: 833-262-8899

Because of the dynamic nature of the Internet, any web addresses or links contained in this book may have changed since publication and may no longer be valid. The views expressed in this work are solely those of the author and do not necessarily reflect the views of the publisher, and the publisher hereby disclaims any responsibility for them.

Any people depicted in stock imagery provided by Getty Images are models, and such images are being used for illustrative purposes only.
Certain stock imagery © Getty Images.

This book is printed on acid-free paper.

ISBN: 978-1-4772-0579-2 (sc)
ISBN: 978-1-4772-2850-0 (e)

Library of Congress Control Number: 2012908586

Print information available on the last page.

Published by AuthorHouse 03/15/2024

authorHOUSE®

Introduction

The path of coming to the knowledge of who I am has not been easy. My understanding (or, lack thereof), sometimes chartered decisions that led to success and other times near-fatal consequences. Through it all, there was no decision that was not divinely used to bring me to who I am today. And each decision started with a "thought!"

Thoughts along the way is a compilation of writings, journal entries and memoirs of life lessons. They are thoughts birthed out of my life experiences, pain, joy, confusion and clarity. From the "Aha!" moments to the Uh-oh" challenges, I became aware that what I think about my experience is what matters most. Sometimes I've had to reexamine my thinking. I've come to understand that my thoughts determine my outcome.

This book serves as a versatile companion, whether used as a devotional or guide. Navigate the Contents page to discover a chapter title that resonates with your thoughts, and make use of the provided pages to jot down your reflections. No matter how you choose to engage with it, I invite you to savor the journey and embrace the possibility that your thoughts may evolve along the way. Enjoy the exploration!

Be blessed!

Acknowledgements

Thanks be to God, my Source! You Father, get all the glory. Thank you for your divine plan for my life; allowing me to have experiences when I miss your instructions. Your love constantly keeps me. I am forever thankful to you and every vessel used to make this project possible!

Mark, my friend and husband, thank you for challenging me. Your unwavering support and the gentle nudges to reach for the best version of myself have been instrumental in shaping the pages within. I am profoundly thankful for your presence in my life. I love you!

To my cherished daughters—Brittany, Brooke, Biannca, and Bryce—your evolving presence in my life is an everlasting source of joy. Thank you for not only keeping it real but also for being consistent pillars of belief and support. Your love and encouragement have been the driving force behind my growth, and for that, I am deeply thankful. Always remember, you are paragons of excellence in every facet of your being. I love you more than words can convey.

I extend my sincere appreciation to Mashiul Chowdhury, the artist extraordinaire, for the captivating tapestry contributions that have adorned the pages of this book.

Special thanks to Greg Johnson for providing the striking photograph featured on the front cover, adding a visual allure to the overall presentation. Your contributions have truly enhanced the essence of this work.

Dr. Gladys Willis; beyond any words, it's the warmth in your guidance that has been a balm to my soul. I am immensely fortunate to have you not only as a source of wisdom but as a beacon of steadfast support, shaping my journey in profound and personal ways. Gratitude fills my heart for the meaningful impact you have made on my life.

Heartfelt appreciation goes to Brenda, who stands as a constant reminder of our rich heritage and unyielding resilience. Your presence, dear cousin, is a cherished connection to our roots, and I am grateful for the enduring bond we share. I love you!

To everyone who will read this, thank you for believing in yourself!

Contents

It's New, and It's All about You!

I want you to think about what you need for this "new beginning." If you press your way to get it, you'll always find yourself "doing" you. Doing you is not a bad thing—although many people will tell you it is. They might say you're self-centered, self-seeking, or even selfish. They may give you ideas and suggestions on how to be less self-absorbed. Doing you means soul searching, investigating, evaluating and recreating, the "You" you want to see. Doing you means getting closer to your creator, for how can you say you love your creator, whom you've never seen, if you don't love the one you see every day? Now, think about it. Whom do you see more than anyone else? YOURSELF. This time, this season, right now —do you!

Your Thinking

The thing you imagine will eventually come into being. Every situation in your life has been divinely set up by your thought process. You may not realize the power of your mind, for whatever you think, you will be. If you continue to think through the eyes of your hurts, you will remain wounded; if you reside in thoughts of desperation, you will remain in need. Now, after all your willful thinking, if you would finally think of things that are true—lovely things, things that are pure, that are honest, that bring good report and virtue—you will materialize a beautiful product that at one time was just an image of your mind. Think about it.

Work

It is extremely hard WORK searching for validation in other people's image of who you're not! Seeking to please one while trying to avoid the risk of wounding another is like WORKing overtime. Stuffing your emotions while others dump theirs (on you) will WORK your last nerve. The next time opportunity presents itself in the way of WORK, stay on your job. WORK out your relationship with yourself; WORK on making yourself happy; WORK out your own soul salvation; WORK on losing the resentments you've gained from trying to do every other job but your own. The pay is so much greater.

Experience

Lessons will come, and lessons will go. Experience is gained by learning the lesson. Instead of asking yourself why the same things keep happening to you, ask God, "What is the lesson here?" If you still yourself enough, you will hear the answer. If you listen to the answer you hear, you will find a solution. If you walk in the solution, you will gain experience. When you gain experience, you will proceed to the next lesson. Tell me, what class are you taking?

"Give it some serious thought!"

(Write your thoughts here)

Praise Break!

Where you are now is a perfect opportunity to Praise God! Think about it. If it's a habit, you've tried, but you can't break it. If it's money you need, unless God releases it, you won't get it. Maybe there's a problem you just can't seem to solve— you know the one where you prayed and prayed, but just kept getting even more deeply involved. Praise is always effective. In praise, you turn it over, you loose what had you bound, and most of all, God becomes readily available to meet every one of your needs. Give God Praise; trust Him—there is no good thing He will withhold from you. Now, go head and Praise Him!

Ever Learning

What are you learning? I have learned that as long as I live, there will be something about me that I must change. I have learned that I can neither make others responsible for my change nor expect them to be bear weights that were never intended for their shoulders. I have learned that not everyone will celebrate, appreciate, or even tolerate my change or the pace with which I change. I have also learned that walking in unforgiveness is like eating poison and expecting the other person to die. I have learned that quality and quantity are like value and amount: similar, but not alike. I have learned, and am still learning, that through it all, God's grace is still sufficient.

Change is Inevitable

Are you still resisting change? No matter how much you try to hold on, change is inevitable.

Here's my story.

While enjoying the fun of jumping against the fast-approaching, brisk waves of the beach, I took notice that most of the participants of this jumping-the-wave frenzy would turn their backs to the oncoming wave, allowing it to gently glide them. My resistance, of course, required that I stand facing the wave head-on. Lo and behold, before I could think again, the robust wave tenaciously seized any bit of control I thought I had, throwing me violently to the left while ferociously snatching my pride and my glory. You guessed it: the doggone water took my wig completely off my head. I'm telling you—change will come.

Relationships

How many of us have them . . .Friends? (Remember that song?) Friends are relationships. What type friends do you have? Examine your relationships. Are they superficial or significant? Do you often find yourself relating to haters, toleraters, or spectators? Do you have relations with appreciators, motivators, and celebrators? Whatever you relationships may be, they are mirror images of who you are. Just for today, rightly relate yourself to the friend you want to be.

"Think about it just a little bit longer."

(Write your thoughts here)

Did You Forget? It's Still New, and It's All *Very Much* about You!

Why must you insist on dragging those people of whom you have been warned repeatedly to let go in this, your new season? You must let them go. I know—I know they're your friend, they were there for you when no one else was, they know so much about you, you've cried on their shoulder, he's your baby's daddy (or she's your baby's mama) and so forth and so on. The fact is, you are not who you were. That needy, helpless, uninformed, and insecure person who needed those unhealthy relationships has now grown into a healthy individual. Healthy things grow, and growing things change. Please let them go. Look at it this way: trying to bring old people into new circumstances is like trying to put a size 8 dress on a size 22 woman. Everything will hang out, and something is likely to bust.

Love, Life

Are you in love, or are you in hiding? If you are happy sometimes and sad most of the time, it's probably not love. Love feels, love deals, and love heals. It does not hide. It identifies issues you resist and accepts what really is, despite your compromise with how you'd like it to be. Love allows an open door for hurt to be released and healed. Now tell me, are you peering through the peep hole, or are you in love? Careful, now. Love is truth, and truth does not hide. Write your loving response.

_____

_____

_____

It Is Finished

Yes, it is finished. Don't be deceived by appearances. The show is really over. All your efforts at trying to make other people comprehend your clarity are complete. You are through compromising, tolerating, and trying to understand and be understood. It is now time that you go—run, even—to that place called "there"—that place you often daydream about yet avoid in your attempt to control everything that is now finished. It's time! It's time for the real you to come out from behind other people's ideas, images, judgments, and visions and walk in your newness. Old things are passed away. Behold! All things have become new. Remember, the past is finished. So what's new about you?

That Don't Belong to You

What do you do when you love someone or something you should not? Remember the old tune *(If Loving You Is Wrong) I Don't Want to Be Right*? The words go on to say, "if being right means living without you, I'd rather live wrong than right." Let's think about that for a moment. Okay, exactly where are we going with this? You're right. NOWHERE. Identify what you love today that just might testify against you tomorrow. If it's so right, then why do you have to do it in secret? Why do you feel so guilty when you do it—or better yet, why do you need more of it to feel adequate? Just be careful, because you may hear those words from Jazmine Sullivan's song: "I bust the windows out your car."

"What were you thinking?"

(Write your thoughts here)

What Is the Exact Nature?

So it happened again. You gave all you had to not even get as much as a thank-you! Again, your devotion and hard work went unacknowledged, and you were treated as if you were obligated to do what you did. Feeling unappreciated and unloved, you press on. Now, tell me something. Exactly what was your motivation in the first place? Did you really expect that a different result would come from doing the same thing? Examine your motives for giving others what you refuse to give to yourself. Today, be fully present for you.

Self-Will? I Don't Think So!

Still working on self-will, huh? *Willing* yourself to do right, *willing* yourself to make better choices. A constant routine of "will powering self" usually runs riot and eventually runs out. When was the last time you sought a higher counsel concerning your life? Have you asked God lately where you're going? What's the next step? Whom shall or should I marry? Will I get hurt again? Remember, the end of self-will usually is disaster. Just for today, turn your "will" over to God and watch "self" evolve in God's grace.

"I thought you changed your mind?"

(Write your thoughts here)

The Right Thinking Means Changing

Your thinking is off. Who you are is not wrong. Your behaviors, however, may need a bit of readjusting. Behaviors do not lie! Many times they contradict who we really are, which leads to thinking that who you are is wrong. Who you are is not wrong, and you are not what you've done—but you are what you think. Remember, if you do what you've always done, you can be sure you'll get what you've always gotten. Change your behaviors, and the result will be a mind transformation. Besides, you never were successful at thinking your way into acting right. So act your way into thinking right. Do the next right thing, and you'll begin to see and know that who you are is divine!

For God's Sake, Just Change!

Stop resisting! There will always come a time when change must take place. Decisions will have to be made, new chapters will be written, others will be closed, and some people may need to be—well—left in the closed chapter. As long as you resist change, you will find yourself dealing with anger, consumed with guilt, residing in resentment, and consequently fearful of everything. When you resist change, you will blame others, find fault, and deny the very fact that you are the one stuck. Change is inevitable and will take place—with or without your cooperation. If you keep resisting change, you may just be the one left behind.

"You should probably think again!"

(Write your thoughts here)

"I didn't think I could do it."

(Write your thoughts here)

Accept and Surrender

Accept and surrender! *Boy, this is a toughie.* Think about it. In most, if not all, of your dilemmas or struggles resides a lack of acceptance and the need to control something or someone. Everybody wants to be in control. Accept that in most cases, you are not! Surrender to engineering what you call the most strategic plan to gain the position of control. The only thing you can control is you (and that, my friend, is a 365-day-a-year job, with no time off, sick days, holidays, or vacation). Accept the fact that some people will never be what you need them to be, and surrender to trying to make them be.

Congratulations (for Showing Up to Life)

You have managed to survive what you call the worst situation of your life. This one was a humdinger. I know you thought you'd never get through, but guess what? *You did*—and I am so proud of you. Now you see that what you went through was purposed, designed, and destined to bring you to the fortified, confident, and satisfied being you see in the mirror today. Whenever you seem to lose your gratitude, think of that situation.

Remember, in the beginning you were blinded by your fears of "what if?," "how come?," and "what should I do?" At one point during your process, you were even ready to give up—but from somewhere, out of nowhere, you got a second wind. You found courage to finish the process. Toward the end, nobody could even tell you were going through what you went through. And now look at you!

You have managed to show up for life—a job well done. *Nobody could do it quite like you!*

Congratulations!

"I'm thinking . . . "

(Write your thoughts here)

Printed in the United States
by Baker & Taylor Publisher Services